I have

SPINA BIFIDA

I have SPINA BIFIDA

Brenda Pettenuzzo
meets
David Purcell
Photography: Chris Fairclough
Consultant: Moyna P. Gilbertson
ASBAH

FRANKLIN WATTS
London/New York/Sydney/Toronto

David Purcell is twelve years old. He was born with Spina Bifida. He has a brother, Ian, aged eleven. They both go to William de Ferrers School. Their father, David, is a company director, and their mother, Ann, is the welfare assistant at a local school. The family live at South Woodham Ferrers in Essex.

Contents

12a Golden Square
LONDON W1

ISBN: 0 86313 562 5

Series Consultant: Beverley Mathias
Editor: Chester Fisher
Design: Edward Kinsey

Typesetting: Keyspools Ltd

Printed in Great Britain

The Publishers, Photographer and author would like to thank David Purcell and his family for their great help and co-operation in the preparation of this book.

Thanks are also due to Mrs Shirley Moore SRN SCM Hvcert, Fieldworker for ASBAH in the Essex area, for her help and advice. The staff and pupils of William de Ferrers School are also thanked.

Brenda Pettenuzzo is a Science and Religious Education Teacher at St Angela's Ursuline Convent School, a Comprehensive School in the London Borough of Newham.

Moyna P. Gilbertson is Executive Director of ASBAH (Association for Spina Bifida and Hydrocephalus)

The early years

"I have always had Spina Bifida. It happened to me before I was born."

David was born on 18th February 1974. It came as a shock to his parents when they saw that he had been born with Spina Bifida. They really didn't know anything about Spina Bifida then. They know quite a lot now! The doctors didn't know at first whether David would be seriously affected or not. He had to stay in hospital for several weeks after he was born.

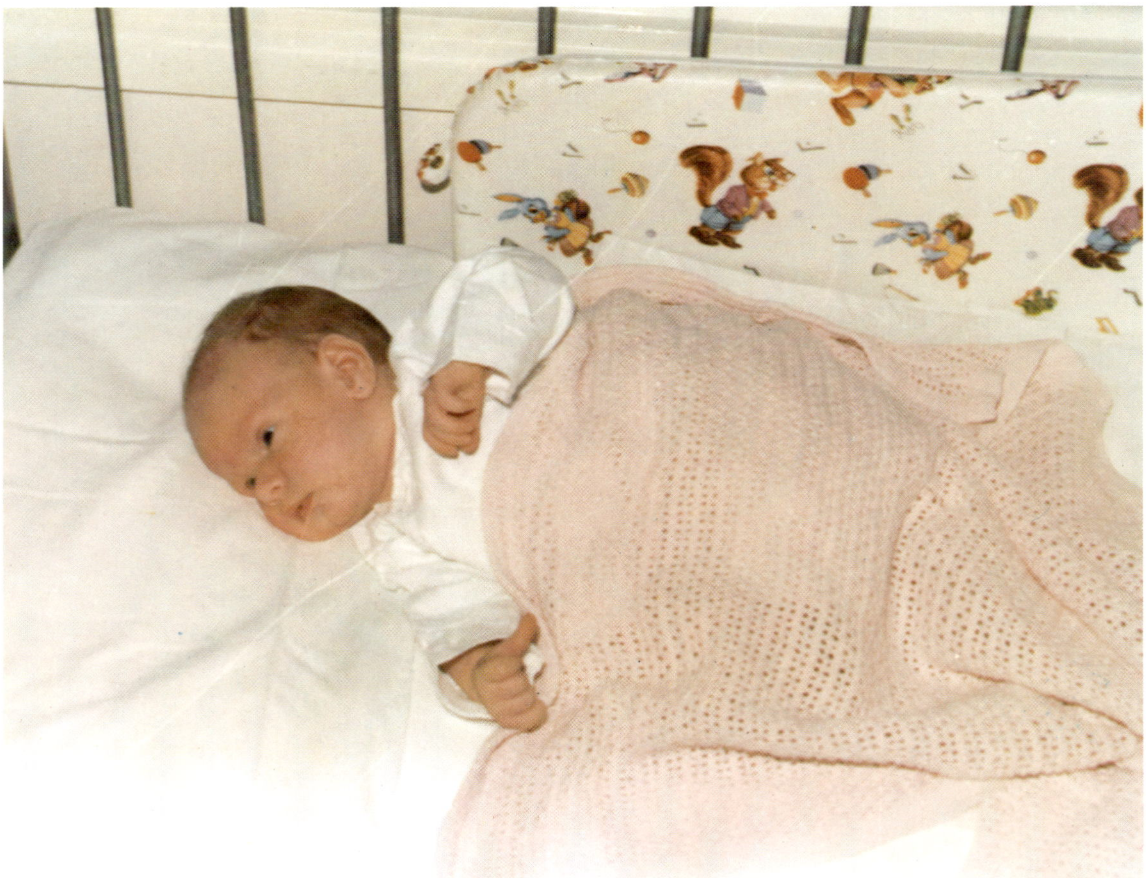

"I had lots of operations when I was young. Most Spina Bifida children have them."

People with Spina Bifida have a fault in their backbones. The bones do not join up properly. This leaves a gap or split through which a blister or cyst usually forms. David's doctors had first to decide whether to leave the cyst for a while, or to operate on him straightaway. They decided to leave things for a while. David went home with his parents but he often went back to the hospital. When he was 18 months old, he went in for an operation to remove the cyst in his back.

"At first, no one thought that I would ever be able to walk."

There are many different ways in which babies with Spina Bifida can be affected. There are so many nerves running through the spine, that no one can say which ones will be damaged. David's doctors did not know which parts of him were not going to work properly. They had to wait and see. When David was two years old, he went back to hospital to have an operation which would straighten his feet. His parents were told that he would probably never walk.

"I did start to walk, soon after I was two."

Not long after he had recovered from his foot operation, David began to stand up in his cot. He then managed to walk around the furniture at home. His parents had hoped that this would happen, but had not imagined that it would be so soon. In fact, he learned to walk so well that last year he had to have an operation to rebuild his hip socket. It was wearing out because walking had put such a strain on it!

Life today

"As I grew older, I began to understand what was wrong with me."

David can use his legs for walking, but only with the aid of his sticks. He does not have much feeling below his knees. He cannot feel his feet. For him, walking feels like he is balancing on his ankles. The sensors and muscles under the feet are needed to keep one's balance. David is unable to feel these while he is standing. He cannot stand still without something to lean on.

"I never know whether my feet are cold. My mum has to tell me!"

Many people with Spina Bifida have poor circulation in their feet and lower legs. David has to be even more careful than most people. His feet cannot tell him when they are getting cold. If any part of our bodies gets chilled, the cells can be damaged by frostbite. David has to make sure that his feet are well protected. He always wears warm socks and in cold weather he does not stay outside for long. He has lots of warm baths, which help to maintain his correct body temperature.

"I love going out on my bike. I've had a BMX for a long time now."

Once again, David surprised everyone including his parents, when he began to ride a bike. His brother had one, but when David wanted a go, nobody thought he would be able to keep his feet on the pedals. Then his uncle adapted the pedals so that it would be easier for David to keep his feet in place. He soon found that cycling was much easier, and faster, than walking!

"I'm hoping to do the cycling proficiency test at school."

Both David and Ian spend a lot of time cleaning and maintaining their bikes. If they do the Cycling Proficiency course they will have to show that they know all about cycling, road safety and keeping their bikes roadworthy. David is more fortunate than many Spina Bifida children because cycling is a valuable form of exercise. It is good for his heart and lungs as well as his legs.

At school

"Ian and I started at our school at the same time. I'm allowed to use the lift, but I usually take the stairs."

David missed some things in Primary school because of his many visits to the hospital. He stayed on for an extra year. Before he went to secondary school there was a meeting about his special needs. His parents and teachers discussed everything with a field worker from ASBAH (Association for Spina Bifida and Hydrocephalus). At school there are Welfare Assistants who will help if David has any problems.

"My class tutor is called Miss Ball. She treats me the same way as everyone else."

David's class is called 1M. In it are about thirty boys and girls. His brother is in a different class, or tutor group. While David is in class he looks no different from the other boys in the classroom. He can take just as active a part in the lessons as anyone else. Just by being in 1M, David has taught his class and Miss Ball quite a lot about Spina Bifida.

"None of us had ever done C.D.T. before we came to this school."

Craft Design and Technology involves many different subjects, all connected with designing and making things. At the moment David's group is doing metalwork. They are learning how the tools should be used correctly. It is difficult for David to manage the tools and to stand up at the same time, but he can cope if he leans on the bench.

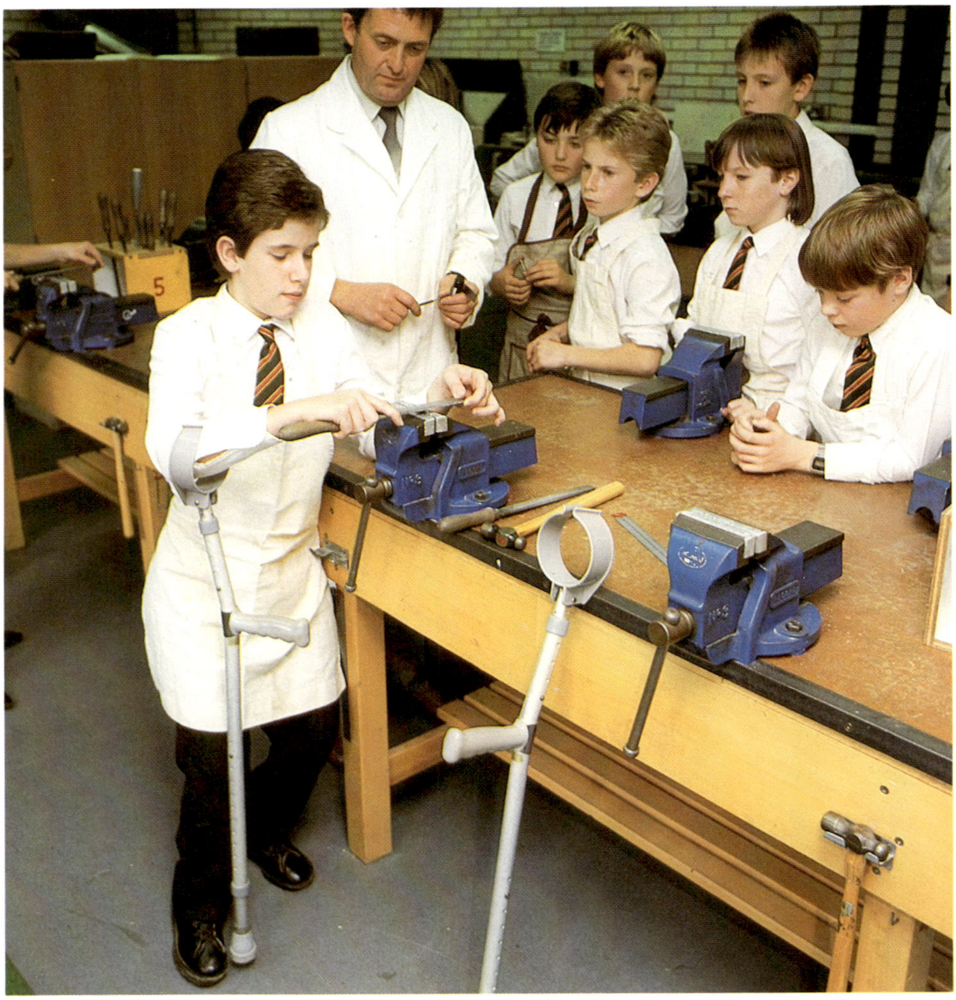

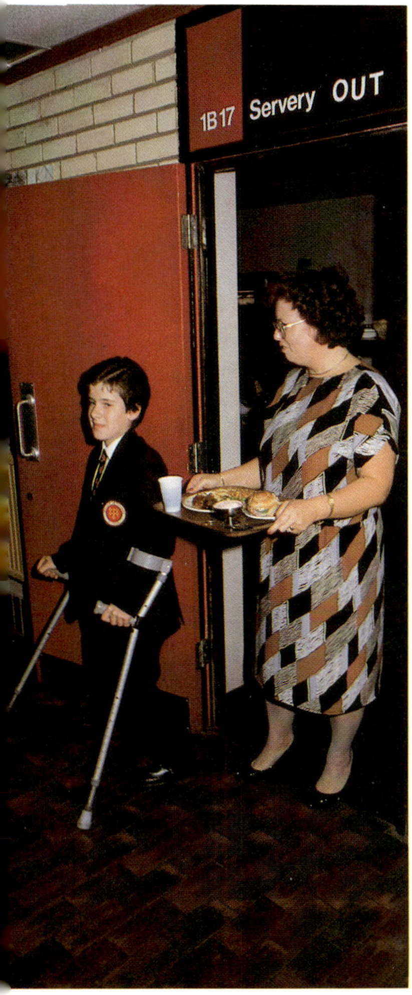

"My school is very large. It would be hard for me to get my lunch without help."

There is a self-service cafeteria at David's school. Pupils have to queue up with trays to get their lunches. David would find this impossible without help from one of the Welfare Assistants, Mrs Liddle or Mrs Oxley. One of them is on hand to help David carry his lunch to his table and take the empty plates back afterwards.

"After lunch I usually have a job to do!"

The lunch-break is only one hour long, and most of that time is taken up by actually eating the meal. For the twenty minutes or so which are left, all pupils are supposed to get some fresh air. It is not easy for David to go outside. He goes upstairs to the medical room to see Mrs Oxley or Mrs Liddle, after he has been to the toilet. They usually have some work for David to do, such as stapling or folding letters, which is very helpful to them.

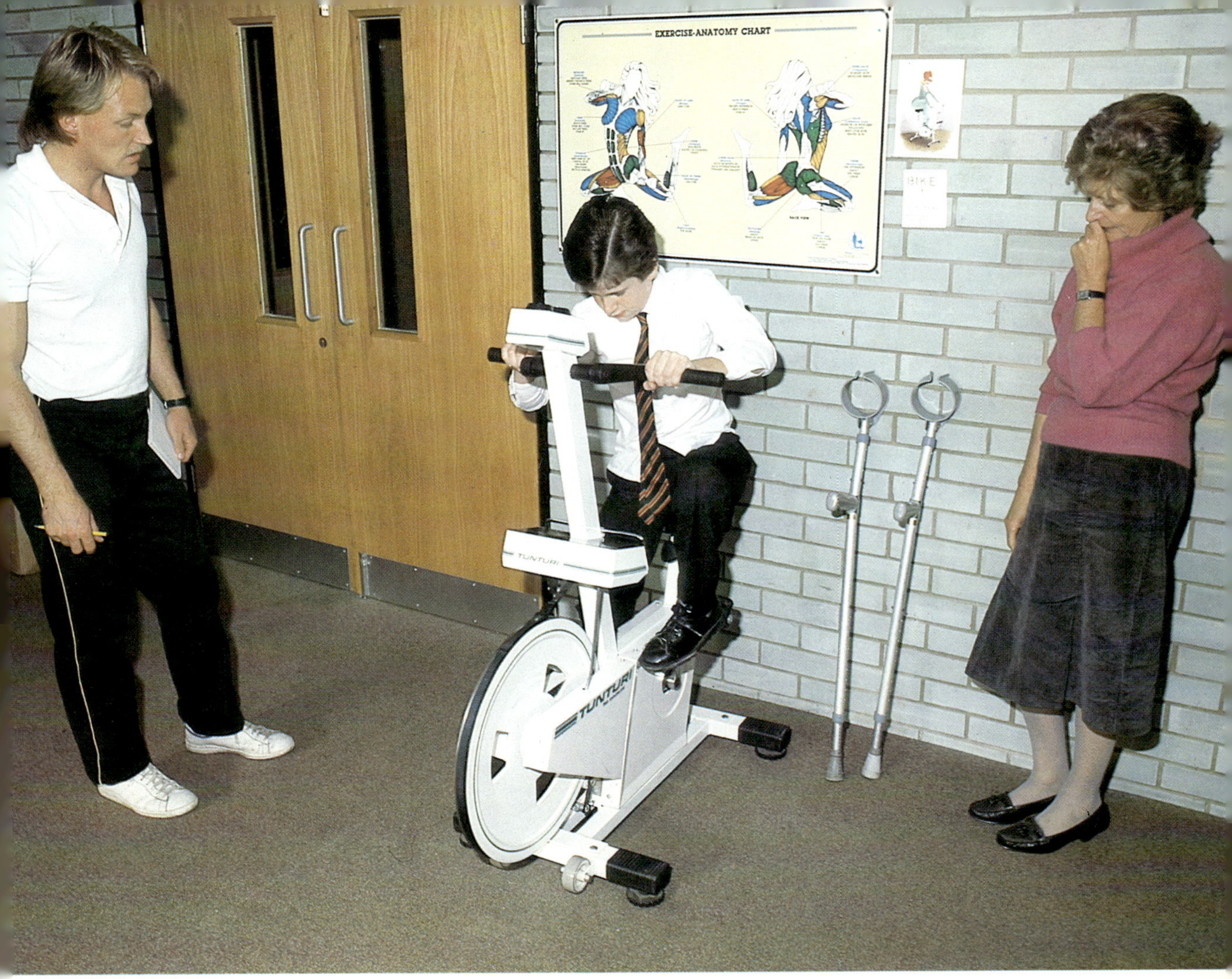

"Mr Moss and Mrs Mason are working out exercises for me to do in the gym."

Mr Moss is David's games teacher. At the moment he is doing games skills with the rest of David's class. David is unable to do many of the things they are doing. Mrs Mason is a physiotherapist. She has come to the school to help Mr Moss work out a routine of exercises in the weights room. There are lots of different pieces of apparatus in this room. Each one can be used to exercise a different group of muscles.

"Mrs Liddle will be able to help me use the apparatus, once the exercises are worked out."

Expert knowledge is needed to design appropriate exercise routines for people like David. By using the exercise benches and the weights correctly, David will be able to strengthen his upper body. He will also do exercises for his leg muscles. The exercise strengthens the muscles that he does use.

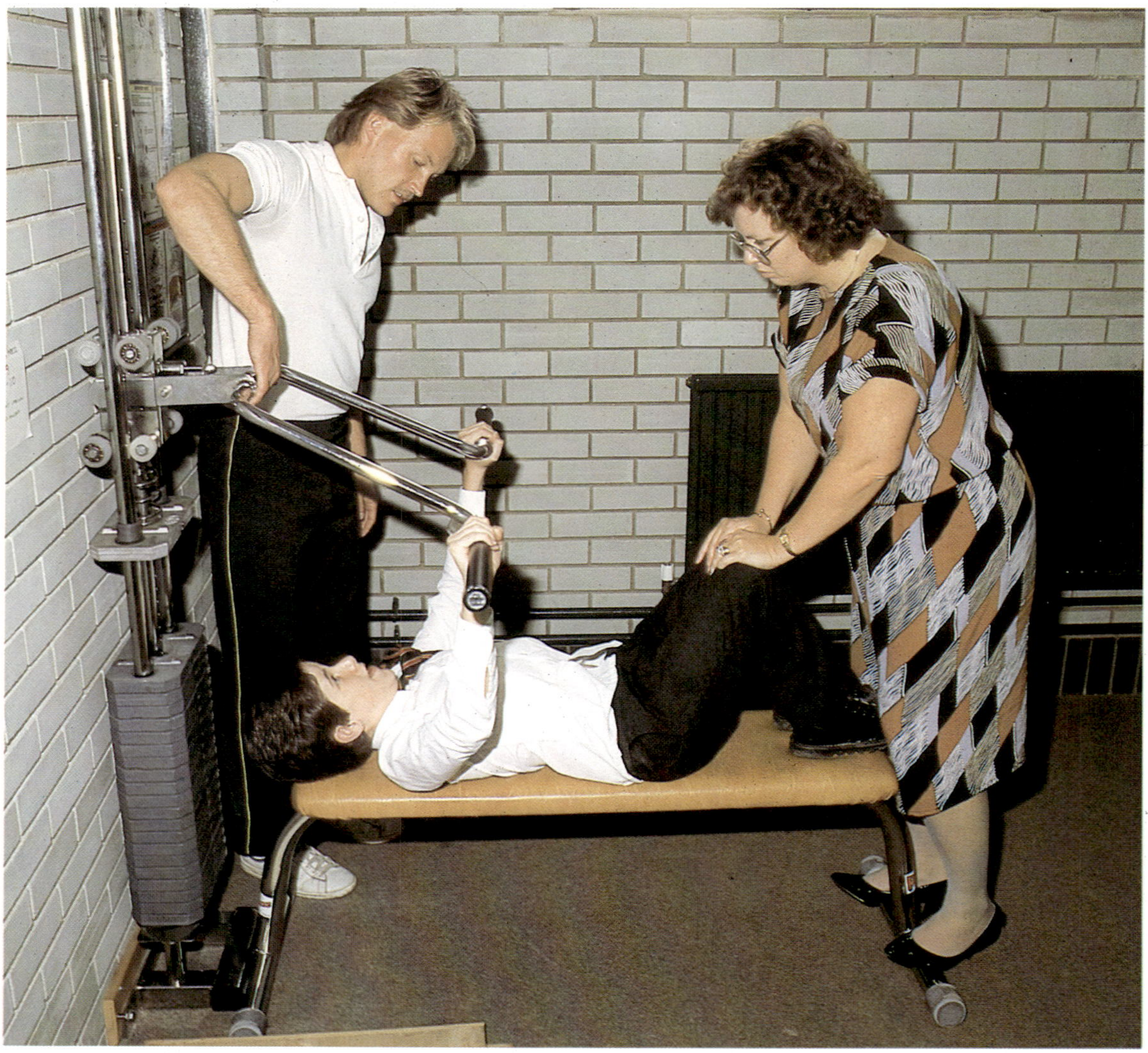

"I have to be driven to and from school, usually by taxi."

David cannot walk to and from school or to the bus stop like most other pupils. It would take too long, and he might find it difficult to manage his school things. In the winter he would get too cold. The taxi solves this problem. Many boys and girls with Spina Bifida, and with other disabilities, get to school in this way.

At home

"I have a bedroom on the ground floor with my own shower room and toilet."

Many people with Spina Bifida are much more disabled than David and live their lives from a wheelchair. Having an extra bathroom built is therefore not uncommon. The bedroom downstairs is easier to reach, and there is a specially adapted shower and toilet. Some families have ramps installed, for wheelchairs to get over doorsteps, and some homes have lifts in them.

"I have to drink quite a lot. This helps prevent infections in my kidneys."

Many people with Spina Bifida cannot tell when they need to go to the toilet. They are said to be incontinent. There are many ways of dealing with this problem and Spina Bifida specialists take great care to choose the right method for each person. David has learned a technique called *self-catheterization.* This means that he can empty his bladder several times during the day. He does not have to worry at other times.

"Every Wednesday we go to a youth club. We get dressed up, especially when there is a disco!"

The youth club is open from 7.00 pm until 9.00 pm each week. David and Ian have time to do their homework before they get ready. David has been able to dress himself since he was much younger. This means getting into a variety of unusual positions!

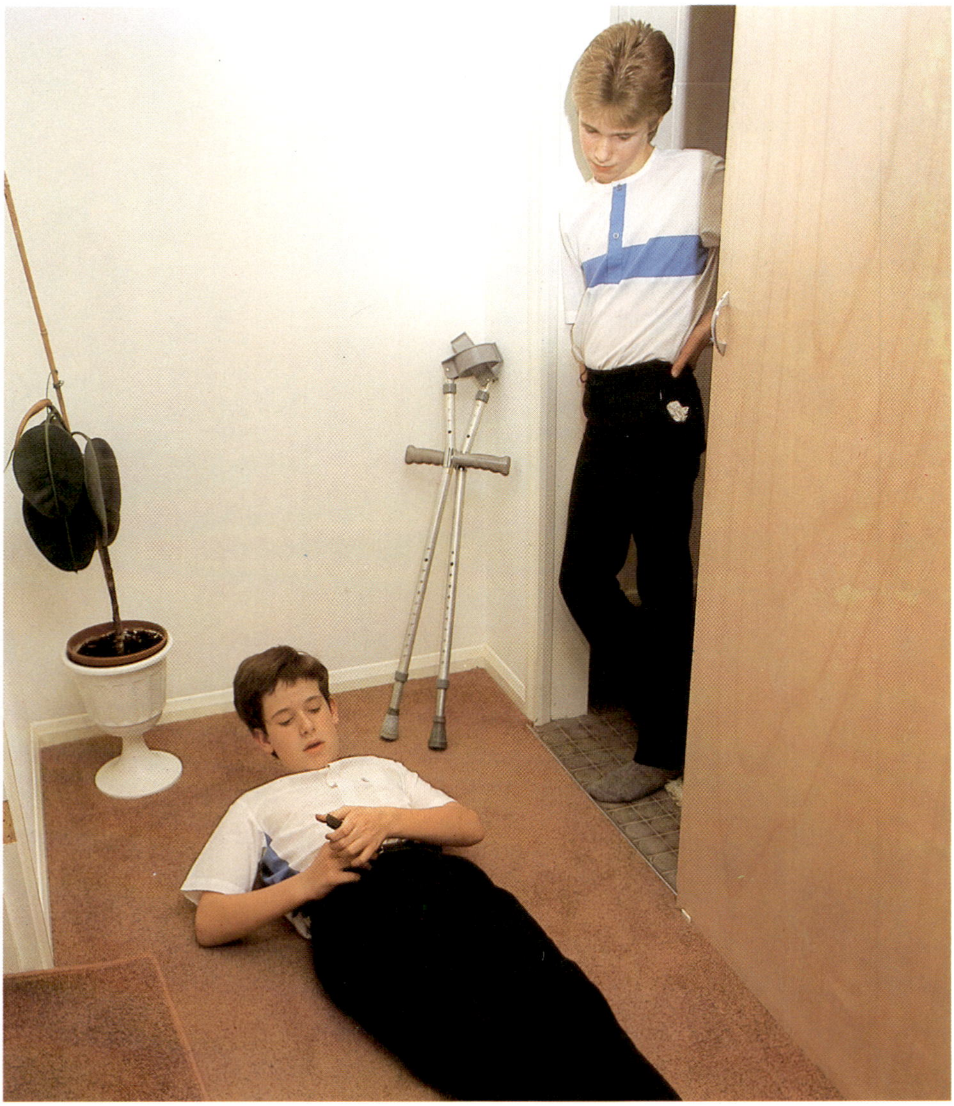

"I read a lot about horses and I've been going to horsemanship classes after school."

David has many opportunities for extra activities after school. He used to sing in the choir at his Junior school. David has joined the choir at his new school. They practise after school on Tuesdays. On Thursday afternoons David has joined a horsemanship class. He is learning all about horses and how to look after them. Eventually he may be able to learn to ride.

"I do lots of things with my family, especially at weekends."

It would be easy to treat David and other boys and girls like him, as if they are very delicate. This would not be very sensible and David himself would not like it. He and his brother are very similar and they are very good friends. David's parents did not know how his life would be affected by Spina Bifida. They are glad that he is able to lead such a full and active life.

Facts about Spina Bifida

Spina Bifida means "Split Spine." It is the most common major abnormality present at birth. The various forms of Spina Bifida are all part of a collection of abnormalities called *Neural Tube Defects*, which affect the development of the brain and spinal cord. Many children born with the other defects do not survive for very long. Children who have Spina Bifida often have a very good chance of leading happy and fulfilling lives.

The fault in the spinal column found in Spina Bifida cases begins during the first 25 days of pregnancy. Many mothers do not even realize that they are pregnant when the fault happens. Many doctors and medical scientists are working at finding a way to prevent Spina Bifida, but they still do not know why it occurs. Current research seems to indicate that there are hereditary and environmental factors at work in the development of Spina Bifida. Couples who already have a Spina Bifida child have an increased chance of producing another one, and there are regional differences in the numbers of children born with Spina Bifida.

In Spina Bifida one or more of the bones which form the spinal column fail to form properly, leaving a gap or split. There are three main types of Spina Bifida. The first type, *Spina Bifida Occulta* occurs quite often and many people never know that they have it until they have an X-Ray. Usually the only visible sign is a dimple or hair growth on the back. Most people with this form of Spina Bifida have no disability at all.

The second type of Spina Bifida is more complicated. It is called *Spina Bifida Cystica* and its visible sign is the presence of a *cyst* which looks like a large blister on the back, covered by a thin layer of skin. If the cyst contains only protective tissues and fluid, then it is called a *Meningocele* and does not usually involve damage to the spinal cord. If the cyst contains nerves and part of the spinal cord itself, then it is called a *Myelomeningocele*. This usually means that there has been damage to the nerves supplying the body below the site of the damage. The result of this is that there is some degree of paralysis, loss of feeling, and very often incontinence.

The third form of Spina Bifida is called *Cranium Bifidum* and is similar to the second form except that it is the bones of the skull which fail to join. In its most severe form it causes serious brain malformations and many affected children are either still-born or die soon after birth.

Many children who are born with Spina Bifida also have *Hydrocephalus*. In this condition there is a blockage of the cavities in the brain through which the cerebro-spinal fluid flows. If the fluid is unable to drain away properly the head will swell and there will be brain damage as a result of the pressure inside the skull. Twenty years ago this condition caused the death of many children within a few weeks of birth. Since 1958 it has been possible to control the fluid by inserting a *shunt* which allows it to drain away harmlessly.

Although there are many people with Spina Bifida Cystica, the effects of the condition are probably not the same in two people. The spinal cord has such a complex structure that it is unlikely that exactly the same nerves would be damaged in two different people. So each Spina Bifida sufferer has his or her own particular set of problems to deal with.

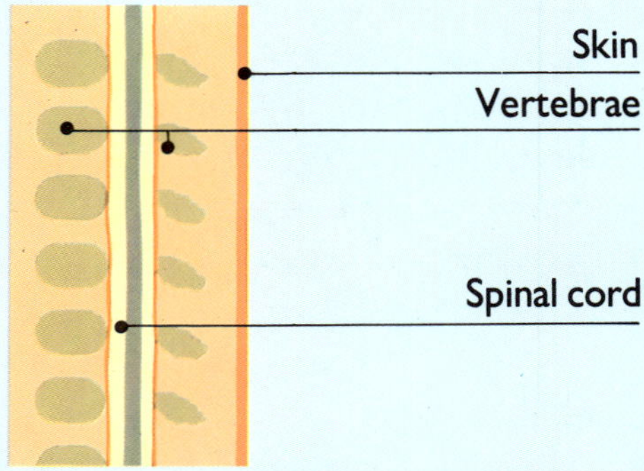

△ **A normal spine**

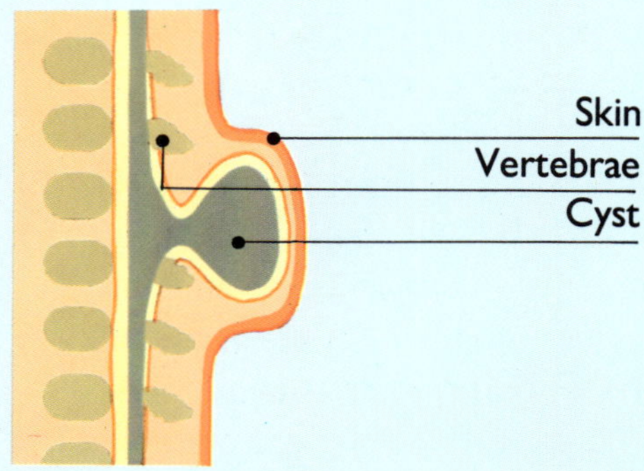

△ **Meningocele.** The outer part of the vertebrae is split and a cyst is present. The spinal cord is normal.

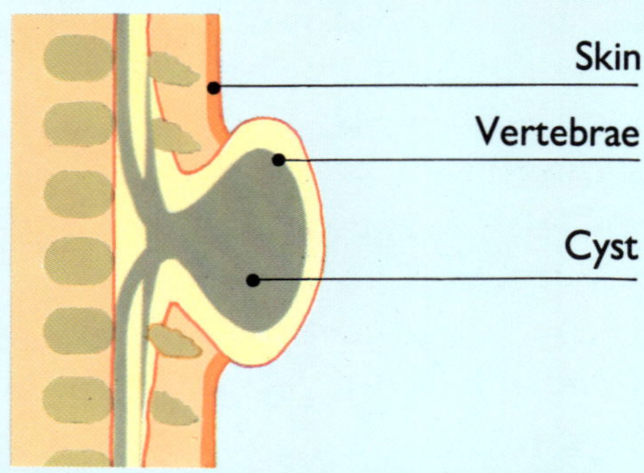

△ **Myelomeningocele.** The outer part of the vertebrae is split and a cyst is formed. The spinal cord is damaged.

People with Spina Bifida are often unable to use or to feel their lower limbs. This can result in several problems. They often have poor blood circulation in their legs and feet, so they must be careful to avoid getting very hot or very cold. Many people are confined to wheelchairs. This means they may get pressure sores. Those who are mobile with sticks, may fracture their bones or damage joints very easily. People with Hydrocephalus have to be on the lookout for signs that their shunt system may be blocked or infected. Parents have to be watchful for these signs in young children. Those who are incontinent have a variety of methods available to them for coping with the problem. In many cases they are able to stay almost completely dry. They must, however, be ready to deal with any infections which may arise in their urinary tract and kidneys. Modern antibiotics and improved methods of orthopaedic surgery have been developed since the 1960's. Many more Spina Bifida children now survive and are able to take their place in society.

The "risk" of giving birth to a child affected with Spina Bifida is about 1 in 250, for a person with no family history of neural tube defects. However, if a couple already has one affected child, the risk is increased to 1 in 25, and for a third child it is 1 in 8. Despite these statistics there is no evidence that parents are "carriers" of the condition or pass it on in the same way as other inherited conditions are passed on.

In the United Kingdom the incidence of Spina Bifida varies from region to region. In the South East the rate is about 2 per 1,000 births. It is higher in all other areas, rising to around 5 per 1,000 in South Wales and 8 per 1,000 in Ireland. Scientists have not yet been able to determine what, if any, environmental factors can explain this uneven distribution of Spina Bifida throughout the country.

At present, about eighty per cent of people with Spina Bifida develop hydrocephalus. Others may develop it without having Spina Bifida.

ASBAH

The Association for Spina Bifida and Hydrocephalus was founded as a national organization in 1966. It provides help and advice to over 80 local Associations in England, Wales and Northern Ireland (Scotland has its own Association).

The local Associations offer support and advice to parents and provide much needed contact with other families. The National Association provides information on all aspects of care and management of people with Spina Bifida.

ASBAH employs Fieldworkers in many areas who liaise with local associations and help families with the strain of caring for a disabled child.

ASBAH supports and promotes research in order to gain a greater understanding of Spina Bifida and Hydrocephalus, their treatment and – most importantly – prevention.

ASBAH is almost entirely funded by voluntary contributions. Details of all ASBAH services and literature are available from:

ASBAH
22 Woburn Place
LONDON WC1H 0EP
Tel: 01-388 1382

Glossary

Catheter A very thin tube which can be used to empty the bladder of urine. This type of tube also has many other medical uses.

Cyst A visible sign of Spina Bifida which is like a large blister on the back, covered by a layer of skin.

Cerebro-spinal fluid The liquid which, enclosed within protective membranes, surrounds the brain and spinal cord. Together with the membranes, this fluid forms a protective cushion or shock-absorber around the brain and the spinal cord.

Hydrocephalus This word means literally "water on the brain" but the "water" is really cerebro-spinal fluid. This can cause problems if too much is produced or if it is not absorbed properly by the body. The excess fluid builds up around and within the brain, and the pressure it creates can cause brain damage if not treated.

Meningocele The least common form of Spina Bifida which does not usually involve damage to the spinal cord. The nerves are able to function and there is often little disability present.

Myelomeningocele The most common form of Spina Bifida and also the most serious. The spinal cord is damaged or not properly developed. There is always some degree of paralysis and loss of sensation below the damaged vertebrae. The amount of disability depends on where the Spina Bifida is and the amount of nerve damage. Many children and adults with the condition experience problems with bowel and bladder control.

Neural tube This is the part of a developing baby which develops into the brain and the spinal cord – the Central Nervous System of the future child. If the Neural Tube is damaged then the brain and spinal cord or some of the surrounding tissues will not form properly.

Spina Bifida Occulta A very mild form of Spina Bifida which rarely causes disability. The visible signs are a dimple or small hair growth on the back.

Spinal cord The part of the Central Nervous System which runs from the base of the brain down to the base of the spinal column. It is protected by the bones of the spine, and by membranes and cerebro-spinal fluid. Nerves from the spinal cord connect it with all parts of the body.

Index